AN ORDINARY MAN'S
EXTRAORDINARY ENCOUNTER
WITH THE HOLY SPIRIT

THE MYSTIC NEXT DOOR

EDWARD JOZSA

To inquire about speaking engagements, or to share your own experience with God, or to obtain additional copies of my book, email:

themysticnextdoor1@gmail.com

or

edjozsa@presenceofGodencounters.com

Recommendations

Captain Ed Jozsa genuinely thanks God for the automobile accident that nearly took his life. Read Mystic and you'll know why. From the horror of the wreck itself and subsequent long and painful recovery, emerges a beautiful story of revelation, grace, and redemption. Ed was given a gift. He was allowed to experience a glimpse of the eternal. A place outside of time and space that Ed convincingly reveals is just as real as our physical reality on Earth. In this powerfully written, inspirational story, Ed describes that place and what it now means to him in the present, past, future, and for eternity…and why he can't wait to go back.

–Daniel V. Ferracciolo, *B-767 Captain,*
Instructor, Standards Line Check Airman;
Former Naval Intelligence Officer,
Lieutenant Commander (select), USN

Having known Ed personally through the community and remembering the horrific accident that nearly took his life, then following up with him in ICU at Methodist Hospital in Indianapolis… Later he would reach out to share personally his "out-of-body" experience in those early hospital days of suffering excruciating physical pain. His testimony will give confidence and hope to those who ever wondered what may lie beyond the boundaries of physical reality. Ed's testimonial book is a must read for anyone who might doubt the existence of God and His eternal world!

– Pastor Andrew Marshall
Victory Chapel Community Church

IN WALKING WITH Ed in his journey, I have come to know that God's message to Ed goes beyond his own personal, extraordinary experience. It is a reminder to all of us that God's presence, action, and loving desire is ever present. The story of this ordinary mystic can inspire all of us.

Fr. Dale W. Ehrman, *Pastor*
Holy Spirit at Geist Catholic Church and
St. John Vianney Catholic Church, Fishers, Indiana

DEDICATION

THANKS TO MY family for their endless support. I want to thank my wife, Amy, for helping to fill in some of the behind-the-scenes details I never knew and for carrying such a heavy burden during my long recovery.

I would also like to thank my three children: Chance, Nate, and Anna, for their strength during this time and for dealing so well with all the changes in their lives.

THE COVER

SOON AFTER I returned to flying, I snapped the photo on the front cover of this book from the cockpit of my 767. As I flew into that beautiful sunset, I could see how the horizon represented the world as I now see it. We dwell in that tiny strip of orange, still yet illuminated by the light of Christ. Above and below that stripe exist two very different worlds. The one below is a tortured pit where fallen angels and the dammed are chained. The blessed kingdom of the Holy Trinity full of angels and saints above extends on forever.

In that faint sliver of light, a battle rages for our souls. The victor of that battle will determine in which world we will reside for all of eternity. The *Miles Christi*, the soldiers of Christ, are the ones who through the power of God and the help of His angels, fight that battle.

TABLE OF CONTENTS

INTRODUCTION

"For I know well the plans I have in mind for you—oracle of the LORD—plans for your welfare and not for woe, so as to give you a future of hope. ¹²When you call me, and come and pray to me, I will listen to you. ¹³When you look for me, you will find me. Yes, when you seek me with all your heart, ¹⁴I will let you find me—oracle of the LORD—and I will change your lot..." (Jeremiah 29:11-14).

In 1944 ALLAN ROBERTS and Doris Fisher wrote a song named "Into Each Life Some Rain Must Fall." In life, as in the song, we hope to have more sunny days than rainy ones, yet we know we will encounter times of trial and hardship. These rainy days can tempt us to lose faith and cause us to wonder: *Is God out there—somewhere—or not?*

Why does God let bad things happen to good people, and why do we need to suffer? The aftermath of "rainy days" can even cause us to ask: "God, are You even listening to my cries and prayers?"

When this suffering comes, consider the following advice of St. Pio of Pietrelcina:

———

What does it matter to you whether Jesus wishes to guide you to Heaven by way of the desert or by the meadow, so long as he is always with you and you arrive at the possession of a blessed eternity?[1]

St. Pio, as well as so many other saints, spoke of how God guides us on a path that leads to Him. In this book, I would like to take that belief a step further. Consider for a moment that God not only guides us on that path, but He also paves it for us brick by brick, carefully constructing it with every trial and suffering we face. With each new suffering, He places yet another paver in front of us that hastens our journey toward Him. He does not use trials alone in the construction of this road. The cement between the stones is His grace and love that holds our path together; however, the suffering is the focus of this story.

As we go along on our journey, occasionally looking back to admire the craftsmanship He used to create our unique road is so important. After all, He designed our path exclusively for us, to make following Him easier. God makes no two paths the same, and sometimes He allows unpredictable bumps along the Way—this story is only a small piece of the one that He has made for me.

To tell His story well, I will need to share about a few of the pavers that the Lord chose to place along my path. You may have already observed from the cover of my book that a car accident was part of my path. On that day I should have died. More than that, I would like to share about three heavenly and hellish visions that subsequently changed my life.

———

This book is true, and before continuing, I want every reader to understand that I am in no way different than anyone else in this world. This story about my path could have happened to any person of God's choosing. Truthfully, I am not sure why He chose me to relay this message. My story is one of God's blessings and miracles—many of which had taken place in my life all along. I was simply too blind to see them.

This book is God's story; He simply gives me liberty to share it with others.

———

[1]"Padre Pio Quotes About Heaven," *Vaticansite.com*, May 1, 2017, https://www.vaticansite.com/padre-pio-quotes-heaven/, accessed January 20, 2023.

———

CHAPTER ONE

MAY 30, 2017; 5:45 P.M.

O N MAY 30, 2017, I was living a good life, and I enjoyed success by the world's standards. I considered myself a decent, churchgoing guy who attended Mass most Sundays, unless, of course, something more important was taking place. I took care of my family, and we enjoyed the friendship of many.

I felt strong, healthy, and even invincible—bulletproof; I didn't think anything could burst that bubble of invincibility. I felt I could do anything, and I would have been the guy most surprised to find out he was dead. More so, I would have been shocked to know that I was on a path that was *not* leading to heaven.

I was driven in life to provide all the earthly needs for my family and myself, and I was laser-focused on that task. I pray that the Lord knows how absolutely ashamed I am of who I was and how I behaved. I'm embarrassed that I believed anything could be more important than Sunday Mass. I'm saddened that I was content to be so poorly catechized. But mostly, I regret neglecting to build treasures in the Lord's kingdom for my family and myself. I was living life by the world's standards—not by the Lord's.

I always considered myself very lucky, but now I know it wasn't luck; rather, my whole life *I had been blessed!* I believed

I was on my way to heaven, but because of the Lord's mercy, I would soon learn how much work I would have to do and how much mercy I would need to enter, God willing, His kingdom.

"What profit would there be for one to gain the whole world and forfeit his life? Or what can one give in exchange for his life?" (Matthew 16:26).

I had been married to my beautiful wife, Amy, for 23 years, and we had three children. Chance, my oldest, was 17. Nate, barely 15, had recently gotten his driver's permit, and my daughter, Anna, was 12 years old. I was working as a pilot for FedEx, flying the Boeing 767.

I had a decent amount of time at home with the family since I had finished my six-month training cycle, so I hadn't flown yet that month. I was on reserve on May 30, which is like a doctor's being on call. That week's reserve started at midnight, and I needed to be ready to go to work at all times. I was at home doing my regular chores—mowing the lawn and even grilled an early dinner to reheat after the kids' track practice that evening.

A few minutes after five o'clock, Amy reminded me the kids needed to go to practice and asked if she should drive them. Because her mother had recently come for a visit, I offered to take them instead. My oldest was working that evening at a ski shop, so only Nate, Anna, and I got in the car. We drove about a mile to pick up a neighbor boy who was also on the team. We backtracked, so we were only a quarter of a mile from our house when I turned out of the neighborhood. At that point, I had no way of knowing my life would take a very drastic turn. As I would soon learn that drastic turn, which would prove to be more than a physical one, was also a spiritual turn I will never forget. To this day, I remain grateful for everything I experienced and endured. I am thankful for every brick and stone carefully placed by the hand of God on my path.

I was facing north, turning west onto 236th Street, a country road in the middle of central Indiana's cornfields. It was planting time in the farm country north of Indianapolis. Not surprisingly, a very large tractor was traveling eastbound on the road toward me. Several cars had been backed up behind the slow-moving tractor going about 15 miles an hour. The tractor also took up most of the road, so I stayed on the far right of the road, even onto the berm to give the driver extra maneuvering room, while driving slowly. Once the tractor had passed my car, I moved back into my lane and started to speed up. In a split second, I saw a sudden flash of black, and then my car exploded.

I would later learn that the flash of black I saw was from a black SUV patiently following the tractor, which had been rear ended by a second SUV. The woman driving the second SUV had been speeding, driving faster than 55 miles per hour. Completely oblivious to the slowed line of traffic, she never took her foot off the gas or braked as she plowed into the SUV in front of her, causing the driver to lose control, cross the lane, and plow head-on into our car as we were passing the slow-moving tractor.

The collision with the SUV was the most violent impact

imaginable. Bouncing and spinning, our car left the road and came to rest in a nearby field, facing our house in the distance. I was dazed and could remember thinking, *What happened?*

I could only see white at first, and I thought I must have been blinded by the explosion. However, when the airbag finally floated down in front of me, I realized the safety feature had deployed and had blocked my vision until it deflated. The fact that no cars had been in front of us or behind us in our lane before the crash left me very confused as to why the car seemed to explode.

I couldn't help looking at our house in the distance, knowing many days would pass before I would see home again. On the other side of the road in another field, I could see a heavily damaged black SUV, and another SUV 150 yards beyond. Of course, I didn't know it at the time, but the SUV that had caused the head-on collision had traveled over 400 feet in the freshly plowed field before coming to a stop.

I tried to turn to see if the kids were all right, but I couldn't move. The neighbor boy, who was sitting in the backseat, had lost consciousness briefly. When he came to, he began yelling. I could see that Anna was already out of the car, using her phone to call for help. I again tried to turn, though unsuccessfully, to look in the backseat. The relief I felt was overwhelming when I saw Nate walk around Anna. I look now in hindsight that their survival was one of the many miracles of this story. Of the nine people and three totaled automobiles involved in this accident, there were no fatalities.[1]

"For he commands his angels with regard to you, to guard you wherever you go" (Psalm 91:11).

Anna called Amy to tell her we had been involved in a bad accident. "Mom, you need to get here right away!" she urged. Amy thought I was fine because she could hear me ask, "What happened?"

With the help of a passerby who had a railroad-sized crowbar, Nate had been working feverishly to free me. Unfortunately, professionals and more powerful equipment would be needed to remove me from the wreckage of my car.

Pinned in the car, unable to move, and confused by the accident, I struggled to breathe. My mind was fixating on trying to figure out how I had gotten where I was. _Is this a dream? None of this makes any sense. This is too sensational to be real-life._

I was in tremendous pain, and I began wondering why I was struggling so hard to breathe. Encased in broken glass and mangled steel, I sat immobile, barely able to draw a breath, and in agonizing pain when I finally realized, _This is real!_ At that moment I noticed my car horn was blasting in my ear, and I found the noise distracting to the intense concentration I needed to breathe.

Meanwhile, other motorists had called 911. One of the police dispatchers, a friend named Brenda, happened to be visiting at a nearby home and saw the accident from the driveway. She called the number of the sheriff's dispatch center directly to notify the emergency personnel to send "everything you have" to the crash.

We know Brenda personally, and she walked across the plowed field to my car. "Ed, help is on the way," she assured me. Her husband Kurt got into the passenger seat to try to help me. A nurse named Cindy who was on her way to work also stopped to help. She didn't leave the scene of the accident until we did. I'm sad that we never did obtain her full name.

Like many others that day, God placed these folks exactly where they needed to be to help me survive. And just like He placed the people on my path I would need at the collision site, God would continue to provide for my family and me repeatedly throughout the coming weeks and months.

After Amy answered Anna's call, she raced to the site of the accident and arrived before the first responders. When she saw the car was so severely crushed on the driver's side, she knew it was very bad and even thought I might be dead. I had been watching her speed down the two-foot drop into the field, and when she came alongside my side of the car, she saw my head move and realized I was alive.

As Amy got out of the car, she saw Anna on her hands and knees praying, while Nate was still working to free me. She returns to that moment with pride, knowing they did everything right and calmly. At the same time, seeing me trapped and the kids in turmoil was heart-wrenching for her.

As best I could, I started to take an assessment of my "prison." I couldn't see the steering wheel that was buried in my chest. I was hunched over it, panting for every shallow breath. The dashboard in front of me felt like an elephant on my chest. The center console was pressed into my right ribs. The door was bowed out from my body's impact and was bent in half. My legs were crushed together in a small circle. The car was in pieces around me, but I was trapped in what felt like a vice.

At one point during the waiting, I had tried to push myself back from the dash with my free arm. Only then did I realize the arm had been broken. I knew my glute had been shaking throughout the time I was pinned in the car. What I didn't know was the shaking resulted from the muscle's holding my femur in place. The impact had driven that bone through my shattered hip socket. That side of my body was no longer on the seat, and while concentrating on my breathing, I was also trying very hard to hold myself together. I needed every ounce of effort I could muster within to keep going.

The accident happened at 5:45 p.m. We live fairly far out in the country, so 20 excruciating minutes passed before the first paramedics arrived. An EMT on his way to work arrived on the scene before his partners in the trucks arrived. Unfortunately, he didn't have equipment in his personal vehicle. He walked calmly up to my car, reached under the hood, and yanked the wires to stop the blaring horn. I was so relieved when the noise stopped, but that respite would be the only relief I would feel for a long time.

After the first paramedics arrived and assessed the scene, they realized I was inextricably pinned inside the wreckage of my vehicle. They immediately called for the Jaws of Life to be transported to the scene. They could only start an IV and keep me stable while waiting for more trucks, men, and equipment to arrive. Meanwhile, they assessed the kids and found all had suffered some type of injury; thankfully, none were life-threatening.

The paramedics were surprised we were all so calm. Amy told them what medications I was taking, what I was allergic to, and what little she knew about the accident. She knew she had to keep her composure.

One of the paramedics jokingly said to Amy, "You're so calm…do you have a large life insurance policy on your husband? Usually, we have to sedate the spouse while the accident victim is screaming!"

His comment brought brief amusement to the tenseness surrounding my condition. I felt immensely reassured that my wife was in charge and would take care of me. Also on scene was another family friend named Brian, who was the sheriff's deputy in charge. Although I wouldn't learn of his presence until a few months later, at the time having someone we personally knew in charge of the scene was reassuring to Amy.

I assessed my injuries as best I could, telling the paramedics about my difficulty in breathing and that very likely my legs and arm were broken. The paramedics stared at me with shocked looks after I had briefed them on my status. The pain was excruciating, but I knew I needed to stay calm and help myself. I had no idea I wouldn't be extricated from the car for two and a half hours. Some of the emergency personnel would later receive awards for saving my life, and I will remain forever thankful for them.

As I waited for the Jaws of Life to arrive, my focus became inhaling and exhaling—simply breathing. Little did I know that for the first two weeks, my focus would be second by second because that is how long I could manage dealing with that much pain. If I had been told I would be in that pain for another minute, I felt I would lose my mind. I kept my sanity only by focusing on the next second: *one more second, I can make it that long.*

Breathing was so hard for me. I had once thought I was invincible, but I now knew I was weak and vulnerable. I was now broken. Still, I knew I wasn't going to die that day. I thought of Art, my 49-year-old pilot friend, who had recently died of a heart attack in his sleep while on a layover. Pinned in that car, I told myself, "Art didn't get a chance to fight. That's not going to be me. I'm not going to go like that."

Though I knew my situation was bleak at best, I had no fear of death. I knew—not a machismo, but a God-knowing—I would survive. A calmness settled over me as I told myself, "I have a chance to fight, and I know I'm not going to die." I know I wasn't in shock or denial. I also knew I was the only person on the scene who believed I would live, but I knew that I was going to live as a fact.

Once the Jaws of Life arrived on the scene, the workers covered me with a blanket and started cutting through metal. However, despite their heroic efforts, nothing was working. Men were cutting and pulling to no avail. Hearing their frustration and desperation at their failure to free me, I would encourage them, "I'm still here. You're doing fine. I'm still okay. Everything's going to be all right." I continued to concentrate on taking my shallow breaths—*inhale and exhale.*

At some point, a bearded EMT approached me and said, "We've done as much as we can. We will need to sedate you so we can pull you out."

"Why didn't you sedate me two hours ago?" I asked. I remember going to sleep then. Once I was completely sedated, four EMTs grabbed me from various angles and repeatedly and violently pulled on me until they freed my body. I fell on top of them and rolled onto the field with my eyes open.

Another neighbor, Paul, had now arrived on the scene, and when he saw me on the ground, he feared the worst and asked, "Is he dead?"

One of the EMTs answered, "He's only sedated. His eyes look lifeless because of the medication."

As it turned out, the fact that I had remained trapped in the car for so long was a blessing in disguise. The doctors later said the metal wrapped around me was like a giant tourniquet. The EMTs and paramedics didn't know that my spleen had ruptured, and more than likely, I should have bled out before ever arriving in surgery six long hours later.

I was loaded into an ambulance for an hour while an emergency helicopter waited in the field. I was completely unaware that a sort of "custody battle" was taking place between the aircrew and the emergency crew who had pulled me from the wreckage. State law did not allow a takeoff until the sedation wore off. Unbeknownst to Amy and everyone else on the scene, the two crews argued with each other for an hour.

Thankfully, the ground crew won the battle for my life, explaining that every second mattered in getting me to a trauma hospital, since I could be bleeding internally (and I was). The aircrew reluctantly agreed to disregard the law and fly me to Methodist Hospital in downtown Indianapolis while I was still sedated. Drivers who crash in the Indy 500 race are sent to this hospital, which specializes in horrific trauma cases like mine. If the medical personnel at the crash site had followed the existing rules, I probably would not have lived.[2]

During that hour-long battle, I remained sedated in an ambulance, and the only ones allowed to see me were the Fire and Rescue crew. My priest, Fr. Dale, arrived at the scene of the accident but wasn't allowed to see me. After the helicopter lifted off, he drove nearly an hour to administer the Sacrament of Anointing of the Sick before I was taken to surgery. How thankful I am that he remained with Amy to provide comfort until the wee hours of the next morning.

While the crew argued, Amy was fighting another battle. Our two children also needed to be transported to the hospital, but the EMTs wanted to take them to the local hospital. Amy explained she had to have Nate and Anna in the same hospital where I was because she needed to be there for me as well. Our neighbors, Troy and Karen, volunteered to drive Amy and the kids to the ER at Methodist Hospital.

On the drive to the hospital, Amy called my close friend and work colleague, Jim, and told him I had been in a bad accident and would not be back to work "for a long time." She asked Jim to please notify the company for us.

Jim called the duty officer at FedEx, another pilot named Mark. Mark removed Jim from his scheduled week-long trip and booked him in a hotel near the hospital for a week so that he could be by my side. Jim met Amy at the Emergency Room and helped out for the next week.

Jim lives in Chicago and had gotten to Indianapolis for work earlier in the day. Amy assumed he was home when she called him and was completely confused, surprised, and relieved when she saw him sitting in the ER, waiting for her. Thankfully, once again, God placed a crowd of friends to help us right where we needed them the most. God would provide an unimaginably large list of friends, family, and strangers who would continue to care for our family over the next three-plus months. To this day I am still humbled beyond words by the charity our family was shown. We could never repay the generosity we were given by so many—even if we were to live for a thousand years.

While all this battling was going on at the scene, my daughter Anna posted a picture of my crushed car with Amy's next to it on Instagram and asked her friends and family to "Pray for my dad." Because of the speed of social media our son Chance, who was at work, was called by a friend in North Carolina before Amy even had a chance to notify him of the accident. She felt terrible that she hadn't called him, but she was so busy at the scene.

Chance drove to the scene and, upon identifying himself, he was allowed to pass the roadblock to get to me. I was already in the ambulance by the time he arrived, but he was there with the rest of our family. Without our knowing, friends in another part of the country were helping us and praying for us.

These were the first of so many miracles and pavers that the Lord placed before me on the path He was leading me on to meet Him.

"My God will fully supply whatever you need, in accord with his glorious riches in Christ Jesus" (Philippians 4:19).

---

[1]The woman who caused this accident had some children in the car with her. Tests later proved she was driving under the influence of drugs.

[2]As a result of my case, Indiana state law was changed to allow aircrews the ability to transport victims who have been medically sedated at the accident site.

— CHAPTER TWO —

INTENSIVE CARE

ONCE I WAS finally transferred to the helicopter, I remember feeling the paramedic's mustache on my cheek as he tried to reassure me.

Through the fog of the sedation, I heard him whisper in my ear, "You're going to be okay." I spoke to him later, and he said he tells that to all his patients. I needed to hear it that night. I have the strange memory of spinning and swinging as the chopper lifted off. In my stupor, I thought the EMTs had put me in a basket underneath the helicopter, and I wondered why they hadn't just put me inside.

I finally arrived at the hospital after nine o'clock in the evening. I was wheeled into radiology for a full-body CT scan to determine where the medical team should start treating me. Frankly, I was in bad shape with compound fractures of my arms and legs. Because of my severe leg injuries, the surgeons didn't know if my foot could be saved.

Both of my lungs had collapsed, ten vertebrae and eight ribs were fractured, and the intercostal muscles between the ribs had been ruptured. These muscles are involved in the mechanics of breathing and helping to stabilize the body. My doctor said he had only seen those muscles ruptured on cadavers and needed to take time to research how to repair them.

"People don't survive these injuries," he later informed me.

I was bleeding all over because of the compound fractures and cuts from shattered glass. The skin had been torn from my back due to the impact, and my hands were bloody and burned from the airbag.

When the doctors realized my spleen had been ruptured, caring for that injury became the top priority. A person can bleed out in 20 minutes from the type of spleen rupture I had suffered. When I was wheeled into surgery, almost six hours had passed since the accident.

Truly, my surviving that long was miraculous—another impossibility in a list that was growing quite long and even longer. The greatest miracle was that I was alive. None of the injuries I suffered were to my brain or spinal cord—yet another impossibility!

After midnight I underwent my first surgery, and I had three more surgeries by two o'clock in the afternoon the next day. In addition to the spleen, surgeons began repairing my left arm, stabilized my shattered hip, and inserted metal bars into my left shin to attach traction for the hip. The surgeons drilled in an exoskeleton on the other leg to hold my foot onto my leg and to keep the bones that remained in place. I woke up on and off, only to be told I was heading for another surgery.

I had some vague awareness of what was going on. I woke up with a breathing tube in my throat that was awful; I was so thirsty. To this day, I carry water with me everywhere I go to quench my constant thirst—a lingering aftereffect from my time in the hospital.

I was also so very hot. I was burning up, so my body was packed in ice to try and cool me down. I was desperate to get the breathing tube removed and the three days of waiting seemed like months—even forever. I communicated with those around me by tapping on a paper keyboard with my right hand. That arm had the least amount of damage and was the only limb not to be immediately repaired.

My right arm would be the only limb that functioned for the next three months. My movement on that arm was restrained with a strap because I kept trying to remove my breathing tube from my throat. I could see the fear on everyone's faces when they entered the room. Whether family, doctors, nurses, or other hospital staff, all looked at me as if they might never see me again. I tried to make jokes with the makeshift keyboard and smile to let everyone know it was still me in that broken shell. Besides, I still had that unexplainable knowledge that I was not going to die, and although I knew it, no one else did.

The breathing tube blocked my vision, and I couldn't move my head to see my own body. Once the tube was finally removed, I took an assessment of me to see if I still had all my limbs. Yes, I saw an arm, a leg, another leg, and another arm! Up until that point, I was afraid to ask if I had all my limbs, and I was greatly relieved to know my body was still intact.

—⁂—

Upon hearing of the accident, Amy's brother Tom, his wife Denise, and my brother Dan, drove separately from Pittsburgh in record time to help take care of Amy and me. Dan and my friend Jim stayed with me in the hospital at night.

Amy and Tom stayed with me during the day, and I insisted they go home to sleep at night, although the drive home was almost an hour. Everyone was much too concerned about me to leave me alone in the ICU because I was pretty incoherent and fighting terrible pain all over. In my helplessness, I needed family there to advocate for me.

The next day, Amy's brother Tom went to the impound yard to see if any personal effects could be gathered from our vehicle. The owner greeted him and asked, "Who was in the accident?"

Tom answered, "My brother-in-law," and the owner responded, "I'm so sorry for your loss."

Tom replied, "Oh, he didn't die."

The owner of the wrecking company was incredulous and said in all the years he had been in the business he had never seen anyone survive a car that mangled. "No one survives *that*," he declared.

Many medical professionals have also told me, "It's impossible that you lived. You should have died in the accident."

In an effort to explain the impossibility of my surviving that accident, some have tried to analyze the why. They offered the explanation that my build was one of the reasons I survived. I had always dreamed of being tall and thin, but God knew what He was doing because a tall, slender man would have died in the accident.

God laid one of the first stones to smooth my path toward Him decades earlier. From an early age, I was driven to work out with heavy weights, with the feeling I was preparing to meet some "unknown enemy." The large muscles I had developed over the years caused my bones and rib cage to thicken, protecting my internal organs from being crushed. And my short frame filled the available space in that car. I was built like a fire hydrant because I needed to be. I don't know how my spleen didn't bleed out, but I know with my injuries, I shouldn't have lived. God needed me to be here, and He was about to give me some gifts to pass along to others.

———

The nurses in the ICU were tremendous. I couldn't even MOVE, let alone stand. The traction would pull me down in the bed, so every hour they would have to pull me back up. The rubber mattress stuck to the torn skin on my back, and when they pulled me up, the bedding would adhere to the wounds on my back. My body began to smell like rotten meat. I hurt so much everywhere, and I would scream every time they moved me. I was embarrassed, but I couldn't stop. Every part of my body hurt, and the skin was ripped again every hour.

I looked forward to the next surgery because I knew when they put me to sleep, I wouldn't feel the pain. When I woke up, I'd ask, "When is the next surgery?" I couldn't think that far out, so I would set the next second as a goal. "I can make it until then." I watched the clock's seconds, minutes and hours go by. I would think to myself, *one more second*, as the days dragged on. I underwent seven surgeries in the first seven days.

Throughout this pain-filled existence, I did experience rare moments of slight relief through humor. For the very briefest of times my mind was given a small distraction—a smooth stone placed to comfort my steps on this journey. One of my friends—a hilarious guy—came to visit me in the ICU, which had all glass doors and walls. I could see him walk into the room next door.

I thought, *Oh, there's Bryant!*

Then I heard him say something like, "Goodness! You look absolutely awful!" (That's the cleaned-up version.) He was not joking, but when he got closer to the other patient, he realized it wasn't me. When Bryant found his way to my room, he said, "You look good compared to the guy in *that* room!"

Another instance that brought much-needed relief was watching my brother Dan slowly eat his body weight in White Castle hamburgers. At the beginning of my ordeal, my friend Andy brought in a 50-pack of White Castles for my family. The first couple of days everyone was much too worried to eat, and as the days went on, no one thought to remove that untouched 50-pack. Later in the week, in the middle of the night, in that darkened room, I heard my brother opening the wrappers of those unrefrigerated little burgers. I was truly worried for his welfare, and I warned him that he would be laying right next to me in the ICU if he kept eating those burgers. This routine would repeat nightly as the week crept on.

It's funny how things that seem so insignificant can have such meaning. I know now that is how the Lord works. What we tend to perceive as insignificant is part of His divine plan. Bryant and my brother provided brief moments of relief during a very bleak existence for myself and everyone involved.

At the time, I wish I could have laughed at those moments.

However, there was no physical laughing for me until I got out of the hospital, and even then, laughing hurt almost too much to be worth it. These brief moments of humor have remained with me. God gave us the gifts of joy and laughter, and these rare moments the first week, were indeed the best medicine.

"A joyful heart is the health of the body, but a depressed spirit dries up the bones" (Proverbs 17:22).

Back to reality, my legs and left arm were completely wrapped, so only my right arm could be used for the needed IVs to keep me going. When the IVs needed to be changed, nurses worked their way up from my wrist to my shoulder, poking around, guided with an ultrasound. I could barely feel the prodding because my body hurt so much everywhere else. Narcotics didn't seem to help much with my pain, but those drugs and others were administered to help me get a little relief. After receiving them, I'd rest for thirty minutes or so, then I'd wait for six hours to get another dose.

I would often wonder how I would ever be able to leave the hospital. The pain was so constant, intense, and so unrelenting I felt as though it would never end. I thought I would need constant around-the-clock care for the rest of my life, and I wasn't sure how that was going to be possible. While I wanted nothing more than to be home, at the same time I was afraid to leave the hospital because I knew my family was not capable of caring for me as I needed.

I spent so much time writing about the severity and complexity of my damaged body and talking about the pain I felt for good reason. Pain is relative, and we all experience it based on our own sensitivities and past experiences. Without this lengthy description, the reader could not possibly frame the pain I was enduring. I lived in a world of pain that I did not know existed. I had no idea that I was about to experience pain at a level that made my current suffering feel mild.

> *"But we even boast of our afflictions, knowing that affliction produces endurance, and endurance, proven character, and proven character, hope, and hope does not disappoint, because the love of God has been poured out into our hearts through the holy Spirit that has been given to us"* (Romans 5:3-5).

CHAPTER THREE

REMEMBERING

A FTER SPENDING A week in the ICU, I was moved to the Step Down Unit (SDU) where, instead of having doctors and nurses all around me, I felt almost abandoned. I was still struggling and in need of prayers. My friend Jim wondered how much I had truly recovered because, during my stay in the ICU, he kept having to repeat what happened to me when I came out of anesthesia.

I'd ask, "Jim, what happened? Why am I here?"

I was heavily medicated, but he'd answer, and an hour later have to tell me again that we were in a bad car accident. Eventually, he started telling me longer, more detailed stories of what had happened.

I didn't want to worry Amy, but I asked her to bring my cell phone in case I needed to reach out for help. My brother Dan and Jim had been staying at the hospital all night for a week, and I convinced them to go home and be with their families. No one had thought about giving me my cell phone before, and up until that point, using it would have been impossible for me anyway. Realizing my struggle, my friend Ming left me his earbuds, since I could not hold the phone up to my ear.

During the first night in the SDU, my physical pain was so bad that I couldn't think about anything else. I was unable to feel emotions like loneliness or even worry because I had to talk myself through every minute of my pain-filled existence. I couldn't do anything to make the pain go away. All I could do was experience it, and pain became my only reality. Every part of my body was in indescribable pain.

Nurses would occasionally ask if I wanted the TV turned on, but the thought of having one more stimulus to process was more than I could take. I felt as if I was withdrawing into my inner self to escape the world of pain in which my body was living. At the time I was aware of this withdrawal, and not until a year later did I understand what had occurred, had happened within my soul.

Amy had gone home, and the hour was late—around eleven o'clock. I stared at the blank wall in front of me as I had done for the past week, trying to avoid any external stimuli. I had lain there for some time when suddenly, a bright square of light appeared on the wall. That bright square seemed to stretch out in front of me like a long hallway. On the other end of that long bright corridor, I could see something in the distance. Then, in an instant, I was there, transported through the light to a place I suddenly remembered.

I realized a memory was being presented to me, but I was living it again as if for the first time. It felt similar to the moment where out of the blue, you suddenly remember a long-forgotten story very clearly.

Things became visually crystal-clear to me. I felt as if my whole life had been spent swimming with my eyes open under murky water. Then rising above the surface, I was seeing clearly with an unobstructed vision for the first time. I understood that everything in my life up until that moment was much like a dream—hazy and fuzzy. Life was like swimming underwater. Life as I knew it wasn't real, but this was REAL. This was FOREVER. I had a profound knowledge and understanding of several ultimate truths, and I understood that these truths are universal to us all. My sharpness of sight was almost disturbing.

I didn't see my body, though I felt as if I were lying on my back elevated a couple of feet off the floor. I didn't feel any pain. I couldn't move, although I could see everything around me. There was no time; I was living outside of it, and I could feel the timelessness.

I was alone—but not like I'd ever been alone before. I knew God had withdrawn from me, and I knew that I had caused the withdrawal. At that moment I understood the truth that God holds our soul in His hand our whole earthly life. I hadn't realized God had been holding my soul until I felt that His touch was gone, and the realization was horrifying. My soul felt bare, naked, and unprotected. God holds our soul in a way that protects it from evil entering from the side or back where we can't see. If evil is to enter our souls, it comes from the front where we can see. We must knowingly invite it in.

"See, upon the palms of my hands I have engraved you; your walls are ever before me" (Isaiah 49:16).

"Even there your hand guides me, your right hand holds me fast" (Psalm 139:10).

I knew someone was with me, but the knowledge gave me

no consolation from the isolation I felt from God's absence. This other presence had neither love nor hate for me, but rather indifference. I felt the presence to the right and behind me.

I have heard that hell is the absence of God. So I asked, "Is this hell?"

He flatly answered, "No."

I then asked, "Is this purgatory?"

With a barely perceptible chuckle of what felt like the pity an adult would give a toddler asking a ridiculous question, he said, "No. This is *forever.*" That chuckle of pity caused me some confusion, but I would later learn that the snicker was the result of my very poor understanding of purgatory.

I knew I didn't want to stay here forever. "How do I get out?" I asked.

He said, "That is up to you."

I asked, "What do I do?

He replied again, "That is up to you."

The presence left me, and fear gripped me as I could now take in my surroundings. To call it *fear* diminishes what the overwhelming and indescribable horror of losing God's presence felt like. The terror was nothing like the fear I have felt in my earthly life.

I was in a cylindrical room with red, shiny doors surrounding me. The red was of the highest gloss imaginable. The wall was made completely of doors of differing sizes, and all the doors had handles that were flush with the wall. Because of not having a body nor being able to move, these doors were of no use for my escape. I looked up at the ceiling, and I was unable to look away from it again, although that is all I wanted to do.

The ceiling was white and translucent with a thick, red liquid—something like blood—slowly rotating in the center, in a motion similar to a slushy machine. As the blood-like liquid twisted around, I felt a painful white-hot burning deep in my soul. The pain felt familiar, yet from a long time ago—like an ancient pain we all know but have forgotten.

I could not place this pain in my earthly life that was more severe than anything possible on Earth. I have since wondered if perhaps it was original sin—something that our souls can identify. If I were given the choice of a lifetime of the pain I knew back in my body or a moment of the loss of God, I would gladly choose a lifetime of pain.

This vision still scares me and feels more real than the life I am living now. The terror was always fresh and new, like being frozen in the moment of being startled by an intruder. The fear and horror never subsided, never diminished, and remained stark and unchanging.

In my horror, since I was paralyzed and unable to respond physically, I tried to think of ways to make the torturous pain in my soul end. I tried thinking it away, using math theorems I'm not familiar with like the large chalkboard problems seen in the movies. I recited poems I never knew before. I performed high-level logic problems that I can't begin to understand now. I recited the classic writings from beginning to end, but nothing I tried worked.

I had access to so much more knowledge than I have now.

Briefly, I had all the knowledge of the world, yet it was worthless to me.

One thing, however, that I did not do was pray. I knew that I could not lift my voice to Him—not even so much that I could not pray, but that I did not know prayer existed. I would later understand that I could not pray because I was no longer with the Lord. I know now that prayer wells up in our soul from God; so without Him, prayer does not exist. Much later, I would study and understand that the souls in purgatory while unable to pray for themselves, can pray for others. They have not lost the touch of God. I understood then why the entity pitied my lack of understanding.

After a time, although time had no meaning, and every moment was like the first terrifying one, I simply stopped trying to escape and leave. I accepted the fact that I would be there forever and that my actions in my earthly life had caused me to lose God's touch. I soaked in my despair, and I resigned myself to my new forever.

Ten seconds or ten years, I don't know how long I was there. I just was. My experience causes me to think about when God told Moses His name, "I AM." I understand now that God always is, always was, and always will be…God. God just is. I was living in that world, and I would always be just as I was that instant; I was misery.

Suddenly, the red liquid within the ceiling started to fade to a lighter shade and yet even lighter. I quickly thought, *what am I doing? Don't stop, keep it up*, but I wasn't doing anything. I had given up trying to free myself. When I realized that fact, the ceiling and the walls crumbled away and vanished. I looked up into the purest blue sky I have ever seen. I was in the lush, tall, and deep-green grass, but I didn't see anything else around me. I felt a strong sense of peace, joy, and excitement.

I knew the being from before was there again, and I asked, "Am I out?"

The voice answered, "You are out."

I asked, "Is this real?"

It responded, "This is real."

Then the memory I was being shown changed from its crystal clarity back to the now familiar fog of everyday life. Then, I saw only black. In an instant, I knew I was back to my old life—back in my hospital bed. It was then that I could remember waking up in the ICU days before, with this memory, but the flashback didn't come to me for over a week after the crash in that SDU. The vision has not faded or diminished in any way since that day.

I'm not sure when this memory is from, but after much contemplation, I believe that the vision originally occurred at the moment the other car crashed into us. As my car spun and bounced, I had a lingering feeling that life as I knew it was not real. The accident wasn't real. My house in the distance wasn't real. It seemed to have a hazy filter.

I could see the accident scene from behind as if I was looking through myself. It felt like I was being pulled out of the mud, stuck in a former place, and looking ahead. I can only describe it as a mystery. The vision was shared with me in the hospital later as a reminder once I could comprehend it more. Having some comprehension of what I saw doesn't mean I understand its hidden meaning though.

Once I understood that I was back in my bed in the SDU, I quickly recalled my first memory of being in the hospital. I woke up on the operating table to unimaginable pain and thought to myself, *It would have been easier to choose death.*

I immediately asked myself, "Did I have a choice between life and death? Was I given the choice to go be with God or to stay here and do His work?" This coherent thought surprised me and lasted only a second. Then the pain overwhelmed me and stopped my concentration. As I looked up into the surgeon's eyes, I saw him turn to someone else and say something. A moment later my eyes closed again.

So much was running through my mind as I looked up at the clock, and I realized it was still night. I hadn't been away very long. I felt as if I had been in that place of regret for an eternity, but in reality, it was only for a moment. For us, 2,000 years from the time of Jesus until today is a long time, but for God it is instantaneous. I was in God's realm, yet I wasn't in heaven or hell. I understood that He exists outside of time while we live within it.

How do our souls exist in time? Maybe our souls were in the mind of God when the universe was born, and that is why we desire to return to Him. Our soul may be connected to God, but we decide what we do here, choosing sin or virtue, and our actions determine where we go after this life. St. Augustine said, "You have made us for yourself, and our hearts are restless until they rest in you."

When I told my priest, Father Dale, my story about a year later, he said that saints have described for centuries how this life is nothing but a haze compared to the crystal clearness of heaven. Now I know what they mean: we are meant to be elsewhere, where we have been and where we truly belong, and where the haze is wiped away.

After this experience of having God's hand leave my soul, I began to feel my own soul and sin, and I can sometimes feel the souls and sins of others as well. God holds each of our souls, so He knows when we allow His goodness as well as the enemy's evil to enter. Each choice we make is a personal one. Our bodies and souls together form our person which is our connection to both the physical and spiritual world created by God. Body and soul are created together by God yet connected to two different realms.

The author C. S. Lewis called us "spiritual amphibians," creatures designed by God to live in two worlds. After our death our body and soul will be separated for a time, only to be transformed and rejoined by God in the resurrection.

But if we are only meant to be with God, what is the point of staying here in this world? Saints including St. Theresa of Avila have struggled with this question, and so have I. I don't know the answer, but I suspect it's to help others along their journey and to help prepare ourselves for our time with God.

"The feeling remains that God is on the journey too."
– St. Teresa of Avila

1) A view of the three cars involved in the accident.

2) Emergency crews on site

3) The heavily damaged driver's side of my car

4) Everything removed to extricate me from the car

5) One of two Lifeflight helicopters sent to the scene of the accident

6) EMTs working with me

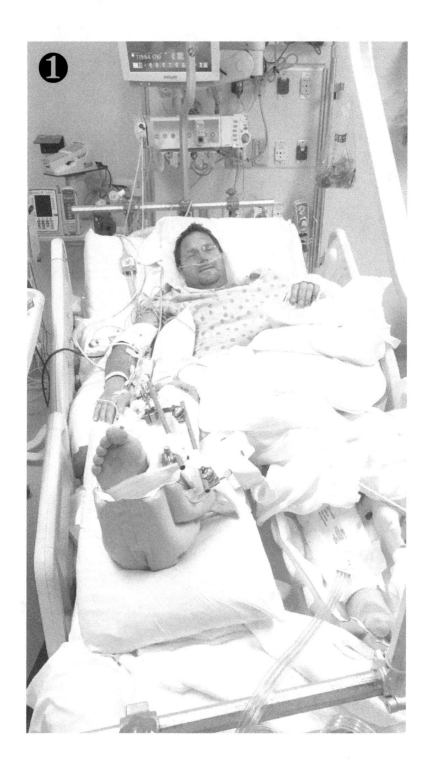

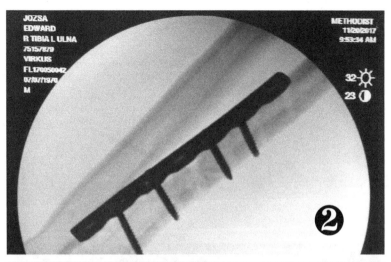

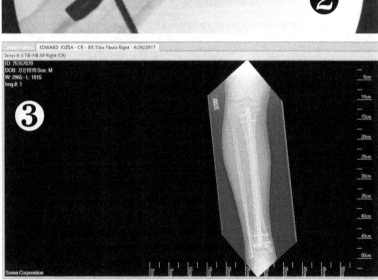

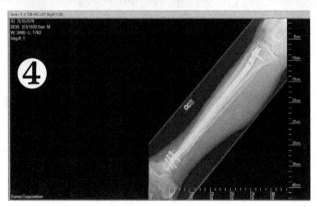

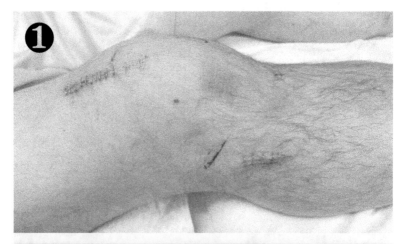

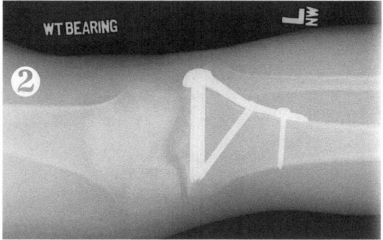

Photos on Previous Pages

1) Ed smiling from his hospital bed

2) Ed's right tibia/ulna with plates and screws to stabilize the bones

3, 4) Ed's right tibia/fibula with plates and screws to stabilize the bones

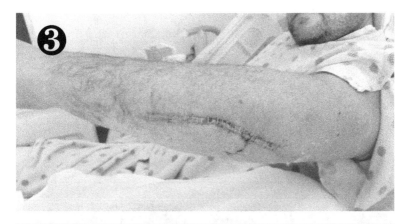

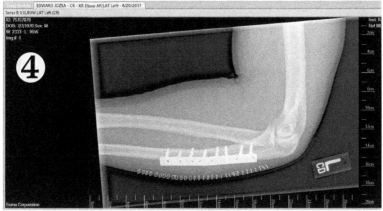

Photos on Adjacent Page

1) Right knee and leg repair; site of a bone graft for his arm

2) An x-ray of Ed's leg showing a repair

Photos Above

3) Ed's left arm, showing his compound repair

4) X-ray showing repair made to Ed's left arm

Ed's repaired hip

CHAPTER FOUR

THE SECOND VISION

I HAVE DIGRESSED. Back to my story. My brother came to my room the next morning as he was preparing to drive back to Pittsburgh. "How was your night?"

After the vision, I was very confused, and I thought that maybe I had died in the crash, and none of this was real anymore. So I lied and said, "I'm fine," but actually, I was wondering if I had brain damage. Then I asked, "Am I alive?"

He said, "What do you mean? I hope so! I'm alive. Yes, you're alive. What's going on?"

I replied, "Nothing. I just wanted to make sure this was real."

I was confused and worried and thought to myself, *I don't think I'm going to heaven.* Now that thought is stark and bone-chilling thought. To know that you have had an otherworldly experience that lasted forever in a place without the presence of God was terrifying.

I realized that hell is even worse than where I went, which was a place of eternal regret and sorrow. The thought of returning to where I had been would have been unbearable, so how bad is hell? That thought was terrifying to consider. On the other hand, I could once again feel God's hand on my soul, and I still feel it today. I don't even have to think about it; I just feel Him always there.

I had heard others talk about loving something with their whole heart. I was familiar with that feeling of being so full of love for someone that you almost overflow with emotion, and I often wondered if I was feeling my soul. The French word for *heart* is *coeur*, and as St. Augustine has said, the heart is the core of our being. I now believe that what people refer to as feelings of the heart are feelings from the soul.

That love you feel for your child, your beloved, or God is felt from the soul. Bishop Robert Barron has said that we can improve our overall happiness simply through small acts of love. Our heart is not simply about superficial feelings or emotions but something deeper. I now know that God's hand is holding all of our souls. God is love, and God created us for love—for Him to love us and for us to love Him and to love one another.

———

My glasses had been shattered in the accident. I reminded Amy after several days that I couldn't see very well and asked her to please bring my spare pair of glasses so that I could read my texts. Reading them from the time of the accident until a week later was so heartwarming. These messages from our friends and family shared thoughts like, "Hang in there! I'm praying for you." "I see your helicopter. You're going to be okay." Even my kids' friends had texted me to say they were praying.

The news about the accident had spread fast and wide; I realized I had benefited from so many prayers from near and far. I learned later that the day after the wreck, my son, Chance, visited three of the largest Catholic churches in the county and placed me on their prayer lists. Those churches added to our own church's prayer list and those of family and friends enabled thousands of the faithful to pray for me every day at Mass. I know the countless prayers offered for me made all the difference and may indeed be the reason God bestowed such awesome blessings on me.

"Call to me, and I will answer you; I will tell you great things beyond the reach of your knowledge" (Jeremiah 33:3).

I didn't tell anyone about that first vision the next day. Amy came in to see me, and I was still really hurting. I asked my brother to call and ask her to bring a rosary. I had one with me in the ICU, but it had been put away during the transfer to my new room. Amy brought the rosary and stayed with me until five o'clock in the evening. Assuring her I was okay, I sent her home to be with the kids.

I was weaning off the heavy narcotics and was miserable. In all honesty, I was getting worse as the day went on. I kept pressing the nurse call button, and someone would answer the call, but no one came to my room to check on me. I waited 45 minutes and buzzed again. When the nurses did their rounds, I told them I was due to receive my pain medication, but as of yet, I hadn't gotten any. The nurse would acknowledge my request, leave my room, but not return, and eventually, I would buzz again and repeat the same request.

Finally, several hours had passed, and I was in more pain

than ever before when a different nurse came in and started to write on the whiteboard. I said, "I'm so glad you're here. I'm so late on pain medications, and I feel miserable. No one is responding to my requests."

The nurse replied, "Did no one tell you?"

I said, "What do you mean?"

He sat down and told me that a mistake had been made, and I been administered too much of a certain pain medication that morning. I needed to wait 24 hours before receiving anything at all, including acetaminophen. "I'm so sorry; the staff should have let you know hours ago. I'm sorry, but there is nothing I can give you."

He stopped what he was doing to sit with me and show true compassion. For a long time, we talked about things unrelated to the hospital. He shared that he was a traveling nurse, and this was not his normal job. "I will be at a different hospital tomorrow, so I probably won't see you again. In fact, you will be home before I come back to this hospital."[1]

At one point in our conversation, I said, "You need to move on and care for your other patients."

"Ed," he responded, "This is all I have to do right now."

After a little more conversation, he left my room to continue his rounds. To this day, I cannot remember his name, and I still feel a certain sadness that I never thanked him for his compassion at such a critical time in my life.

"As each one has received a gift, use it to serve one another as good stewards of God's varied grace" (1 Peter 4:10).

———

Returning to my solitude, I realized I had thought I was in pain before. I hadn't wanted anyone to touch me, but this pain was leaps and bounds above all that I had already experienced. I didn't want to tell Amy because I knew she would worry, and she wasn't sleeping much as it was.

I felt the pain increasing minute by minute. I remember trying to fall asleep, knowing I probably couldn't, but hoping I could pass some time sleeping. I know that the clock had passed ten o'clock when I finally closed my eyes.

Suddenly, I was gone. I was not asleep; I was somewhere else. I hadn't moved, but I felt as if I had opened a window and peeked outside. The first thing I noticed was depth; I could see deep and far ahead. I was looking out into an abyss as if I was looking over a ledge. Below me, lying together, were greenish-yellow reptile-like creatures. They had multiple eyes and mouths, and they were covered in blood. These creatures were wailing, moaning, and making horrifying sounds.

What I was seeing wasn't a normal shock experienced while watching a scary movie; instead, I felt a soul-crushing fear. I believed I could have been looking into the pit of hell, and I knew the creatures to be demons.

I saw the vision when I closed my eyes. Of course, I was so afraid that I opened my eyes, and the vision disappeared. I was still grounded to the earth, and the sound had disappeared. "I must have brain damage," I concluded.

I closed my eyes a second time, and the vision was back. The sounds and the vision were as intense as before, but this time I remained long enough to truly observe the horror below

———

me. I opened my eyes and started praying to Jesus, being sure not to even blink for fear of returning to that horrific place.

I asked Christ to send the Holy Spirit to help me and for Him to remove these images so I could rest, but I had little faith. I was afraid to close my eyes again because I didn't believe the Holy Spirit would come and save me. Since I was too afraid to close my eyes; instead, I talked to Jesus about His Passion. I told Jesus how I never understood how much pain He had endured for us, that He was innocent, and that He didn't deserve any of the sufferings He willingly endured for us—for me. I was so desperate because the pain was so beyond my endurance that I asked Him to take my pain and carry it for me.

Then I immediately said, "No, Jesus. You've already taken my pain once. For me to ask You to carry my pain again is so unfair. I will carry my pain, and I will offer it up as a sacrifice for the salvation of the world."

I would have another vision much later that would explain that I should offer my suffering for the lost souls of this world. This prayer was a foreign idea to me that I would not understand until much later, but it wasn't foreign to St. Paul, who penned the following:

"Now I rejoice in my sufferings for your sake, and in my flesh I am filling up what is lacking in the afflictions of Christ on behalf of his body, which is the church" (Colossians 1:24).

I continued to talk to Jesus about the Passion. "I understand that Your hands and feet were pierced; my bones have been broken, and they pierced my own body. I understand your body was scourged. My back is bloody, and my skin is torn." I finally realized how much Jesus had suffered for me. He hung on the cross for hours, fighting for each breath, trying not to suffocate. I now understood that fear, and I remembered fighting for each breath for hours while I was trapped in the car. I understood that the Lord was just giving me a small taste of the pain—only what little I could tolerate—He had endured for my salvation.

I watched the clock and prayed for about an hour. I didn't see Jesus during this time, but I felt that someone, perhaps my guardian angel or another messenger, was helping me communicate with Christ because I felt someone was responding to me. I felt as if I had help correlating my suffering and understanding Jesus' suffering in a way that was beyond my ability to do so on my own.

I now understood why the apostles dropped their nets and followed Jesus because I was compelled, as I'm sure they were, to be with Him. I asked for the Holy Spirit to come. Then I said, "I'm going to try to close my eyes and rest." I realized then I had forgotten my fear; it was gone.

I closed my eyes, but this time I was looking into the depth of space. Once again, I felt as though I was looking through a window, but this time I could see immense depth into a vast, vast universe. Placed right in front of me was a brilliant sphere of light.

I immediately opened my eyes because I knew I had brain damage. I reached for the nurse call button. As I was reaching down to grab it, an audible voice on my left in my very small room said distinctly, *"It is the Holy Spirit; look at it."*

I looked next to the bed where the chair was. No one was there! In my mind, I could clearly hear, "I'm brain damaged." I reached for the call button again.

The voice I heard this time was also in my mind, speaking in a compassionate and almost pleading tone. I remembered this voice from long ago. I knew this voice from my youth, and I knew it spoke truth.

"It is the Holy Spirit; look at it."

Trusting the voice now, I closed my eyes and looked at Him. Then I was transported to be with Him in a place that felt like space. I felt as if I was traveling away, outward from my body. As I would later meditate on this encounter, I knew that I had not left my body; rather, I had gone deep into my soul where the Holy Spirit resided. And my soul was far vaster than I had ever imagined.

> **"Each of us has a soul, but we forget to value it. We don't remember that we are creatures made in the image of God. We don't understand the great secrets hidden inside of us."**   -St. Teresa of Avila

As soon as I saw the light the second time, all my pain was immediately gone, and I had no memory of it. I just felt wonder, awe, and peace. I was looking at the Holy Spirit, and He was stunningly beautiful. At about my eye level, I saw a brilliantly bright solid ball the approximate size of a large grapefruit. As I got closer to it, the sphere grew to an enormous size. Then I realized the ball had been large all along and only appeared smaller due to distance.

Around Him was a thin veil that had been pulled into four points, creating gossamer spires from the top, bottom, and both sides. The veil looked like a fog all around it. These four spire points created a perfectly formed symmetrical cross, blocking enough of the bright light to allow me to gaze at. Words cannot express how absolutely beautiful it looked or how it felt.

Much like how words could not describe the horror of the other visions, again the words of humans are much too ineffectual to describe God and His glory. I could feel the love of God touching me like we feel the sun's heat on our skin. I could physically feel God's love touching me.

I was aware that I had exited time once again, but now I was enveloped in a forever where I was overjoyed to reside. I felt as if I was a child peeking under a Christmas tree, looking for my gifts. I wanted to see around it, so I looked all around, and I could see it from all sides, and then I came back to face it head-on.

Then I could see what I was gazing at wasn't just light. Little black spots were moving inside it, letting me know it was alive. That crystal-clear vision I had possessed in the red room returned with clarity in this realm. My vision was so much stronger than normal, but before the sight had been painful; now it was appreciated.

I had also gained so much knowledge. I knew the Holy Spirit had the knowledge of the universe, and He was allowing it to permeate into me. I understood that only because of the

Spirit did I suddenly know so many things. Because of our limited human intellect, we refer to many things about our Lord as "mysteries." However, in the presence of the Spirit, I understood all these mysteries. Sadly, much of this understanding did not return with me.

Scripture passages flooded me. My first thought was, "Oh, my, it's not hard at all for God to pass a camel through the eye of a needle." I understood that I was in the presence of absolute unquestionable, unlimited, vast power. I realized with this power, truly anything is possible. I felt His power washing through me as I could feel His love. I knew that power passed through me and to the edge of the universe instantaneously. I genuinely realized that having the faith of the tiniest mustard seed could move a mountain.

We needn't have an abundance of faith because His power is so unlimited. I also knew that there is no battle between God and the devil. That battle is over and done. God won handily, no questions asked. I understood how ludicrous it was to think anyone could win against this Presence. I recognized that nothing could defeat this Power, and I was shocked that the enemy, with his elevated intellect, could not understand what I, a mere mortal man, did. I knew the battle fought now is between man and the devil—not between God and the devil. God is the Master and King of all His creation.

I understood how the Holy Spirit could guide the wise men to the site of the nativity because only those who needed to see, would see the Holy Spirit, as the Christmas star.

I thought of the monstrance that we use to adore the

Blessed Sacrament, Christ's Body, Blood, Soul, and Divinity, and how it resembles what I was witnessing: the brightness of the Holy Spirit with Christ residing in the center.

I also had a better understanding of the Holy Trinity. I used to think of the Trinity as three separate, yet divine, Persons, but now I see them as all in one. When I saw the Holy Spirit, I knew He was a part of God. God wasn't showing me His face nor was I in heaven, yet He was revealing His Spirit to me. Physically touching me within the power of the Holy Spirit was the love of the Father and the mercy of the Son. I could feel all of Him touching me through the Holy Spirit.

I was in awe. I couldn't feel any personal emotions; I only felt the overwhelming love, mercy, and power touching me. His power was so great that if God chose, He could lay waste to the universe as easily as blinking an eye. Such a small output of effort, and it would be gone. He had created the universe just by speaking.

My friend, what can you create with your word? I was studying Him, and I wanted to look at Him forever. I felt like I was home, and I realized I had been homesick my whole life up until this moment, but I never knew.

As I gazed upon Him, one of the spires stretched out toward me. I watched it come to me and come to where my chest should have been. It was going toward the place where my soul resides. When He touched my soul, I felt everything. I felt what I would later learn Teresa of Avila called the Prayer of Union. I felt my soul pouring into Him, and at the same time, I felt Him pouring into my soul. I was falling into Him, and He was falling into me. I can only like the sensation to climbing a steep hill on a roller coaster, and the resulting feeling when the coaster starts to descend, only magnified infinitely.

As I have already mentioned earlier, I know of no words or language to adequately describe experiencing God, and the following words are almost sinful because they do such an injustice to God. I instantly felt love, compassion, mercy, joy, hope, ecstasy—every good feeling in the universe. And I remember the only thing I could say was, "MORE."

This may sound insensitive, but I was so singularly focused that I no longer cared about anything else. I wasn't even worried about my family, whom I love dearly. All I wanted to do was feel this forever. I only wanted to be with Him and never turn my eyes away from Him. I had no worries or concerns at all. I felt blissfully content. I felt like the union was intensifying the longer I was connected. I don't remember its ending.

I woke up in the morning, and the vision was gone. I had miraculously slept the remainder of the night pain-free. I don't even know if any of the nurses came in to check on me. When I woke up, it was light outside—probably around seven in the morning.

The next day, the deeper knowledge I had known was gone. At times now when I pray or meditate, I feel a special union with Him, but far more diminished than in the vision. I can still feel His hand on my soul and bask in His light. I sit still and feel Him. Sometimes, if I feel the union right before I fall asleep, a rush of knowledge jolts me awake, but then it's gone again.

"God is light, and in him there is no darkness at all. If we say, 'We have fellowship with him,' while we continue to walk in darkness, we lie and do not act in truth. But if we walk in the light as he is in the light, then we have fellowship with one another, and the blood of his Son Jesus cleanses us from all sin" (1 John 1:5-9).

I didn't share this vision with anyone the next day because I thought others would think I was crazy. The first visions had details that were harder to recall, but this one was extremely clear and memorable. Nonetheless, I still doubted its veracity and wondered if what I had experienced was real. I spent a lot of time testing out other theories to see if anything could account for the visions.

I was in the hospital for eleven days—seven days in the ICU, two days in the SDU, and two days in a regular room. I was then transferred to a rehabilitation hospital, where I'd spend another seven days. I was unable to move on my own, and an ambulance was needed to transport me. When the paramedics were transporting me to the ambulance, one said, "I can't believe you weren't paralyzed."

Up until that moment, I had never given the possibility of being paralyzed a second thought. Although I could not move my body as a whole, I was able to move small parts, and we knew my spine was intact. I pondered the miracle that saved me from not only certain death but a lifetime of paralysis. I also pondered the amazing events that I had witnessed since the crash.

Only one recurring word can be used to explain my recovery—*miraculous!* When I entered the hospital on May 30, Amy was told to expect me to remain there for a long while. When I entered the rehab hospital, I was told to expect to stay for more than a month. I would return home 18 days after the day of the accident!

Months later, I would reflect back on all three visions, and I would realize that they were the first instances where I could see the spiritual battle in my life. I understood how that battle influenced decisions throughout my life. At either the beginning or the end of each vision the Lord showed me, I heard a voice tell me that it wasn't a vision from God, but rather, it must be from a damaged mind. The enemy was working feverishly to get me to discard what I had seen. I can now clearly see the battle between the angels of light and the angels of the enemy. That very warfare constantly rages around us all.

This battle resulted in my doubt for a year as I tried to determine if this all really happened. I thought perhaps a paramedic may have had parts of conversations with me. I talked to the people who had been at the scene of the accident and asked if they had said anything else to me or if they had heard me ask something like, "How do I get out?" I tried in vain to prove that none of this happened.

Then a buddy of mine gave me a book on near-death experiences written by a doctor who wanted to prove they were false memories. After the doctor had completed his research, he was converted. Of all the experiences the doctor studied, the children's near-death experiences were particularly convincing to him because their stories didn't change over the years, nor did their memories become fuzzy with age.

I finally decided that I needed to talk to my priest, Father Dale. I was fearful that when he heard my story, he would slap me across the face and call me a blasphemer. But what I feared would happen was the exact opposite of what happened. When I shared my vision with Father Dale, he told me my experiences were very similar to those of Saint Teresa of Avila, and he gave me a copy of her book, *The Interior Castle*, written in 1577. Her mystical experiences were so similar to mine, and her description of the Prayer of Union with the Holy Spirit was exactly what I had experienced. After I read and studied the correlations between our stories, I finally concluded that my experience was real.

Over time, I've determined that perhaps sharing my story with people who are sick, in crisis, or maybe just on a spiritual journey, may help them in ways I don't understand.

I have a tremendous sense of peace in my life after experiencing God's touch. A great sense of peace exists in all of our souls. This is the redeeming part of my entire story. I am grateful for the devastating wreck in May of 2017. While I might not want to go through it all again, I am thankful that the accident happened.

My children were injured, and my family has been traumatized for years. As I continue to have surgeries and chronic pain as a result of my injuries, my family has also suffered financially and emotionally. Yet we have received blessings greater than all the strife.

I have no anger toward the driver who harmed us. Many say that's a miracle in itself. I'm thankful for the opportunity to live my life in a way that is pleasing to God. I received a second chance at my physical life and a second chance at my spiritual life. This book is the story of my redemption, but I began to wonder what I was supposed to do next. I started feeling a nudge in my soul.

"Jesus said to him, 'Have you come to believe because you have seen me? Blessed are those who have not seen and have believed'" (John 20:29).

———

[1] In remembering the events of these traumatic days, I have often wondered if this traveling nurse was perhaps the hospital's angel; he was tall and fit and had such peace about him. I know even thinking that possibility probably sounds crazy, but I know he calmed and soothed my spirit that night.

CHAPTER FIVE

THE NUDGE

Y EARS HAVE PASSED, and I still haven't recovered completely. Doctors have told me that the remaining
damage is permanent, and I will never fully recover. I've un-
dergone a total of 22 surgical repairs so far.

Coming to terms with the visions I saw and sharing them
with some close family and friends took me about a year. I was
relieved to receive positive reactions because I honestly didn't
know if even my close friends would believe me. Before long,
a constant urging weighed heavily on me, but I was unclear
about what direction that "weight" was pulling me.

When a close friend faced a crisis, I received clarity. At the
moment of that phone call, that weight I had been feeling lifted. I knew I needed to share my story with my friend and his
wife. Soon, I met another family in crisis, then another, and yet
another.

The need to share always started with a nudge to my soul to
speak of our Lord. I learned that He would provide the words,
but I had to agree to speak to them. Word has spread, and now
I share my story more broadly in my church circles. I've started
to talk with individuals, families, groups, and churches of all
denominations. I've even graduated to using the Internet and
social media to try and get out God's message. I've written this

book—all to satisfy the urge He has placed in my soul, to speak to others about Him.

As part of my sharing and reflecting, I asked myself, as did many others, "Why would God choose to reveal these mystical visions to *me* and to allow *me* to experience the prayer of union with the Holy Spirit?" I couldn't comprehend my worthiness to receive such a special gift.

A friend started calling me "the Mystic Next Door" because I'm just an average guy. Most people would look at me and think, *no way would he have mystical experiences!* The truth is, I know we all experience hearing from God's messengers or receive miracles in our lives, yet we are often reluctant to believe they come from the Lord, let alone share them with others.

At these moments, we second-guess ourselves and question God's gift: "Will I be believed? What will people think of us? Will we lose our friends? Will our family avoid us? I greatly feared the answers to these questions and many others.

As I prayed about these worries, the answer finally came to me. What any person thinks of this ministry or me doesn't matter! Doing what God asks me to do is all that matters. If more people were open to listening to, obeying that nudge He has lovingly placed in their hearts, and sharing both the everyday and extraordinary miracles in our life, imagine how our world could and would change. How might our perspectives change?

I still don't know why I lived when I should have died and why I have experienced so many miracles. I believe I was given a choice to live and carry out God's work while the car was still spinning. Have I learned anything worth sharing? Is there more to my story? I have been asked these questions, and the answer to both is "yes."

Two other significant spiritual experiences helped shape my faith life decades before that near-fatal car crash. As remarkable as they are, I didn't think of them again until I was flat on my back in the hospital, experiencing the miracles God placed in my path. After much thought and contemplation, I started to understand the Lord speaks to us through a gentle nudge and a quiet whisper.

> *"Then the LORD said: Go out and stand on the mountain before the LORD; the LORD will pass by. There was a strong and violent wind rending the mountains and crushing rocks before the LORD—but the LORD was not in the wind; after the wind, an earthquake—but the LORD was not in the earthquake; after the earthquake, fire—but the LORD was not in the fire; after the fire, a light silent sound. When he heard this, Elijah hid his face in his cloak and went out and stood at the entrance of the cave"* (1 Kings 19:11-13).

LIFEGUARD DUTY

W HEN I WAS 16 years old, I was employed for my second summer as a lifeguard at Raccoon Creek State Park in Beaver County, Pennsylvania. This open water beach ran about 235 yards along the shore and extended 50 yards out into the lake. On the weekends, we frequently had more than 5000 visitors daily.

I was working one of those busy midsummer days. Seven lifeguards were on duty at any given time, six in chairs and one walking the beach. As you can imagine, watching that many people for the entire eight-hour shift was incredibly taxing, but we learned techniques to keep track of everyone, constantly scanning from section to section.

We were taught to look at a small section, pause and scan, then move our gaze to the next small block. Look, pause, scan, repeat—for eight hours. The problem with tracking everyone was not only the crowding but also the constant noise. From my seat on the lifeguard chair, the nonstop hubbub sounded as if everyone on the beach was screaming.

We were midway through the day when all my training was suddenly required. I don't know why or how I spotted her, but a young girl, maybe seven years old, was screaming like the other thousands of kids packed shoulder to shoulder near her. The difference was that she was looking directly at me and urgently yelling at me. First, she gave one long scream. Then I saw that she was holding the elbow of a sunken child's arm with one of her hands. The other child's arm was only an inch above the water.

The lifeguard chairs were spaced 50 yards apart, and although I blew my emergency whistle to signal the other guards, they never heard me over the noise of the crowd. I leaped from the chair deck into a full sprint and ran into the lake. The young girls were about 25 yards ahead of me in five-feet-deep water, obviously very deep for their height. I ran most of the way down the beach and into the shallow water, finishing the distance by swimming with my head above water, so I could keep them in my sight.

I saw that the elbow the other girl was holding had already turned a blueish purple, but the rest of her body was hidden under the dark, murky water. When I reached the submerged girl, I pulled her up and swam her out. She was small, slender with sandy, blonde hair, and appeared to be about the same age as her friend. I never learned her name, but I still wonder about her today.

The beach area was comprised of a large ten-acre incline of grass, and at the bottom was a strip of sand running the length of the swimming area. After I ran with her into the grassy area, I placed her on the ground, started my evaluation, and then I began CPR. By this time, a lifeguard who had been on a break and a park ranger had noticed the commotion and had reached the scene.

During my evaluation, I found that the girl had no heartbeat, and she wasn't breathing. She was a horrible shade of blue, and I could not get a clear airway. Nothing I did solved that problem. When I tilted her head to open the airway, I could see water filling her mouth. I then pushed on her abdomen to expel the water from her stomach. A small amount of water came out of her mouth, and I then began the breathing maneuver again. I didn't see any more water in her mouth, but I could tell her airway was still blocked. Nothing I was doing was getting air into her lungs.

I was in a state of absolute panic. I was a 16-year-old kid, and a little girl was lying dead in front of me. All I could do was scream in my mind, **"Help me, God! Help me!"**

In response, a calm, clear voice spoke to me inside my head. He said, "Put her head by the water."

I continued without comprehension, begging Him silently, **"Help me, God! Help me!"**

My panicked urging and the gentle voice repeated our dialog several times until the voice grew firm. He said, "She is full of water. You cannot push it out, but the slope will help you drain it out. **Put her head by the water!**"

I stopped working on her to follow the command, but the ranger grabbed my shoulder and said, "You must continue CPR until the ambulance arrives!"

I screamed the message about the slope and the instruction to point her head toward the water. The ranger helped me move her down the slope. I began the clearing maneuver again, and this time water welled up and flowed out of her mouth like a river. I was amazed at the amount of water leaving her body. Her heart had not been beating for several minutes, though I still am not sure how long. Before I did anything else, she coughed! To a lifeguard, the sound of a cough from a drowning victim is pure music. If a person is coughing, he or she is breathing.

The girl's skin color rapidly turned pink, and she started to cry. The park ranger scooped her up and carried her to the first-aid station, followed closely by her family. I rolled over to sit dazed and exhausted, looking down at the ground. I didn't realize that a huge crowd had gathered around the scene. I felt a pat on my back, and someone said, "You did a great job!"

Another and another spoke the same words of encouragement. Several people mentioned how calm I had been.

I felt like a fraud. I wasn't calm; I was panicked. I hadn't saved her, the voice I heard had saved her. *The voice…what was that?*

I sat still for a few minutes longer, then I went to find the ranger. I felt I owed him an apology for screaming at him in front of everyone. By then, the ambulance had arrived, and the girl was safe with the emergency paramedics. As I approached the park ranger, before I could speak to him, he stepped toward me and shook my hand. "I'm proud of you," he said.

"I'm sorry for yelling at you."

He looked at me with a puzzled look and said, "What do you mean? You were so calm and in command. You knew exactly what was wrong, and you were 100 percent right. You never once raised your voice."

Mystified, I thanked him for the help, and went back to work, worried that everyone would find out I was a fraud. More importantly, I asked myself again, "What was that voice?"

Another 20 years would pass before I would hear that still, calm voice speaking to me to save my own child's life. Ten years after saving my child, while my broken body was lying in that hospital bed in Indianapolis, I heard the same voice pleading with me to look at the Holy Spirit. I knew that voice, and I knew it was speaking truth. I have since learned to listen for the voice and to obey it.

As I contemplated the meaning behind those long-ago events, I was reminded of another significant spiritual experience from decades before when another paver was laid to groom my path to God. Only a few years after I pulled that little girl from the murky water, this event took place near my hometown.

"For by grace you have been saved through faith, and this is not from you; it is the gift of God" (Ephesians 2:8).

CHAPTER SEVEN

THE CRUCIFIX

A FTER ONE OF my many surgeries, two years into my recovery, during Holy Week (the week before Easter), I was reading a book by Sister Anne Catherine Emmerich, titled *The Dolorous Passion of Our Lord Jesus Christ,* which was the basis for the film, *The Passion of the Christ.* Sister Anne spent an entire Lenten season in the 1700s receiving visions and experiencing the Passion of our Lord as a spectator.

The first night after this surgery on April 15, 2019, I decided to use only over-the-counter pain relievers, with the intention of offering up to Jesus any additional suffering I might have during that Holy Week. As expected, I had difficulty sleeping, so I read the book throughout the night. When I came to the part in which Sr. Anne described Jesus' appearance on the cross, I suddenly remembered a dream I had when I was 19 years old, after a local miracle had occurred.

In 1988 the Holy Trinity Catholic Church in the small town of Ambridge, Pennsylvania, requested that a crucifix be restored by my cousin, a parishioner and a skilled local artist named Dominic. The original crucifix statue was very large and very old, dating somewhere between the late 1800s or early 1900s. Dominic agreed to do the restoration work pro bono.

During the work of restoring that statue, I remember visiting his house often as our families were close. During one visit, I went to the garage to see the work he had already done. I was impressed by its size, as well as the unusual feature of Jesus' eyes being open. Dominic began sharing the difficulty he was having in mixing the correct colors for Jesus' eyes. "Ed, doing this restoration work is especially meaningful to me because I've never seen a crucifix before with Jesus' eyes open."

Before Easter week of 1989, the newly restored crucifix was installed above the altar. The priest and congregation were pleased with Dominic's restoration. During the Good Friday service, the most somber service of the year when the church focuses on the suffering of Jesus, the altar boys noticed that the statue was different than how they remembered it. Jesus' eyes, which had been open in both the original and the restoration, now appeared to be closed!

Dominic was in attendance during the Good Friday service. After the service, the altar boys informed their priest of what they saw, and he called Dominic to the altar to ask him if he had painted the eyes closed in the restoration. Dominic replied that he had spent a considerable amount of time trying to match the original pigment used for the eyes. "The eyes were sculpted open, and most certainly, they could not be painted closed."

Dominic proceeded to place a ladder next to the crucifix and climbed up to inspect the statue. He was amazed that the eyes could no longer be seen because the eyelids were tightly closed. The statue was physically different—not only in how it had been painted but also in how it had been sculpted!

While all this was happening, another parishioner, not knowing what was happening, pulled the priest aside and informed him that he had received a message from God during the service that he relayed: "People are going to come from all over to view My image. Do not get upset with them; welcome them."

Once word got out about the change in the statue's eyes, people did indeed come from all over to see the crucifix with the now-closed eyes of Jesus. I recall for the church to remain open for all who wished to see this phenomenon was a major inconvenience.

My girlfriend then, who is now my wife Amy, and I waited months for the crowds to die down, and finally we stood in the long line that wrapped around the exterior of the church to get a glimpse. When we finally reached the statue that had been hung high above the altar, the crucifix was very hard to see. I wanted to see proof, either way, of a miracle.

That night after viewing the crucifix, I had a dream. I was in the church, climbing a ladder to look more closely at the statue of Jesus hanging on the cross. I wanted to see the proof of His now-closed eyes. After I climbed the ladder, I noticed an unusual darkness around me, and I became somewhat unnerved. Once I reached the top of the ladder, I realized I was outside—no longer in the church. I could see baskets, crates, and tools on the powdery, sandy dirt below me. I turned to look at the statue and saw that the ladder was now resting on a real wood crossbeam of the cross—not the artwork that hung above the altar.

I looked back at the statue of Jesus with confusion because

my remembrance was a pristine, clean porcelain figure of a man; instead, the body was filthy and bloody. The thick, curly hair on Jesus was caked with blood, sweat, and dirt. The body of Jesus was battered beyond recognition. His face looked like a bruised, bloodied, swollen, disfigured mess covered in sweat, and his head was lowered. He was more muscular than most of the depictions I had seen. His shoulders were thick with muscle, and his arms looked strong. On the few areas of his body not covered in bruises and blood, his skin had an olive complexion that was now ashen in appearance, grayish as if from lack of blood flow.

In the dream, He lifted His head and turned toward me. The sky became dark. I knew the darkness was from an eclipse like no other, and I was only inches away from viewing Jesus on the cross. His left eye was swollen completely shut; only a small slit of his right eye could be seen. Bloodied mud coated His short curly beard. Though wracked with great pain, He used His arms and legs to lift His body and draw in a labored breath.

He then spoke in an agonizing roar as he exhaled and said, *"Why are you persecuting Me?"*

The sight of Jesus so disfigured and tortured struck fear into my heart. I quickly scampered back down, nearly falling from the tall ladder. I awakened suddenly, sweating, my heart pounding, and my mind racing. I remember thinking, *That was Jesus!*

He was frightening to look at—worse than the most depraved horror movie imaginable and tortured beyond any human limit. He didn't look like the Jesus painted by the Old Masters in serene settings. Sister Anne described Jesus in exactly the same as I saw Him in my dream some 30 years before I read her book.

His words haunt me to this day. I wondered what He meant when he asked, "Why are you persecuting me?" These were the words Jesus spoke to Saul on the road to Damascus before his conversion (Acts 9). I doubted that the Holy Spirit would come to take away the vision of hell, and for a year, I doubted that the visions I saw were real. *Was my faith too weak? Was He speaking to every sinner?* I don't know the answer.

As I contemplated my long-ago dream and Sr. Anne's description of Jesus on the cross, I decided to try to sleep a little before dawn.

I got into bed, closed my eyes, and remarked to myself how beautiful the stars looked. I immediately realized the strangeness of this thought because I was in my bedroom with my eyes closed. I knew that something spiritual was happening, but unlike my other visions, I was not mentally transported anywhere. I could hear my wife's gentle breathing next to me, and I could hear the whirring of the ceiling fan above me. I knew I was still grounded on the earth. As before, I opened my eyes and the vision vanished, but when I closed them again, the vision returned. I kept my eyes closed until the vision ended.

In the vision, I saw countless stars against a very black sky. Occasionally, a streak of light, like a bright shooting star, slashed across, connecting one star to another. I was reminded of illustrations demonstrating the firing of the synapses in the brain to communicate with each other. I watched the beautiful sky for a few minutes, and then the stars subtly changed. At once, the stars were all covered in a fine veil that diminished their brightness. I understood that the stars represented souls, and they looked similar to my vision of the Holy Spirit but much smaller and much less bright.

Since my vision with the Holy Spirit, I have experienced new understanding while meditating and praying about certain meanings of Scripture and my experiences. I feel that God is explaining His truth in a way I can understand when I'm ready. During this vision, I experienced a glimpse of understanding, a wordless lecture if you will, and I understood that while my original intention to offer up suffering to Jesus was good, I needed to understand more fully what God wanted from me and perhaps from others.

In the hospital, I offered to carry my pain for the salvation of the world, but now I understood that Jesus already carried that pain for all of us. The world was granted God's salvation through the Passion of Jesus. I saw that some of the souls I was looking at represented lost souls, and my prayer intention should be for the salvation of those lost souls.

At this point in this wordless lecture, I could hear specific words from the same voice or messenger that told me how to save the little girl. "You must *rescue* lost souls." I comprehended the meaning of the word rescue with a flood of understanding, but I didn't know the short, powerful word the voice spoke in a language foreign to me.

I was helped to understand that the "you" was not only me

but all of mankind—because of the monumental size of the task. If the souls of this vision were represented by the countless stars in the sky, so many souls, who could yet be saved, were, oh, so far from God.

I thought back to the rescue of that little girl and how similar this request was to that moment. I was guided to see her submerged in the murky water, and I was able to bring her to shore. I knew the Lord was the One Who saved her—not me. I merely brought her to where she could be saved by Him. Perhaps that is how we all are to participate in the rescue of lost souls. Jesus called Peter to be a fisher of men—to bring them up from the depths into the salvation of Christ. He calls every believer to do the same.

After this silent message was delivered, I contemplated the lesson and continued to watch the souls. Not all the souls made contact with each other by means of the magnificent streak of light. I was seeing a metaphor of God's soldiers reaching out and leading souls to Christ's salvation through a powerful contact.

After a little while, the souls faded into a background mist, much like a curtain of fog. They became harder and harder for me to see until they were gone. I lay awake the rest of the night, trying to pronounce the divine word that I understood the meaning of. I wondered how someone goes about finding lost souls and pulling them to shore.

I know that some people can be saved with prayer while others need prayer as well as being reached in a meaningful, tangible way. The Holy Spirit often directs us to act in a manner that can reach others and change their hearts. I've been called to share my story, listen to others tell their stories, and witness what God has done for me. In doing so, I hope to draw them (and me) closer to Christ and His salvation.

Months later, my friends lent a book to Amy and me that described how Saint Padre Pio offered the daily pain of his body (that was marked with the five wounds of Christ) up to the Lord for the salvation of lost souls. This book confirmed the importance for me to pray and act in a way that allowed God to work through me. We all are to help rescue lost souls, as well as to help individuals who are faithful, but who may be fearful, anxious, angry, or suffering in some way.

As Paul says in the letter to the Romans:

"I urge you therefore, brothers, by the mercies of God, to offer your bodies as a living sacrifice, holy and pleasing to God, your spiritual worship" (Romans 12:1).

Of course, I know Jesus, the Good Shepherd, is pursuing lost souls. I am only allowing myself to be used to help in the divine effort. I'm content to be a sheepdog who helps the Shepherd tend to the sheep.

"If a man has a hundred sheep and one of them goes astray, will he not leave the ninety-nine in the hills and go in search of the stray? And if he finds it, amen, I say to you, he rejoices more over it than over the ninety-nine that did not stray. In just the same way, it is not the will of your heavenly Father, that one of these little ones be lost" (Matthew 18:12-14).

I am attempting to unify my will to that of the Father. Therefore, my will is that not one soul is lost if there is an effort I can make to help. His will for us is following the Great Commission (Matthew 28:18-20) to which all Christians have been called.

Then Jesus approached and said to them, "All power in heaven and on earth has been given to me. Go, therefore, and make disciples of all nations, baptizing them in the name of the Father, and of the Son, and of the holy Spirit, teaching them to observe all that I have commanded you. And behold, I am with you always, until the end of the age" (Matthew 28:18-20).

CHAPTER EIGHT

LESSONS LEARNED

URING MY MONTHS and years in recovery, I have come to some realizations that I wish to convey. I believe these perceptions will provide some context to my experiences.

I believe the voice I've heard through the years was a messenger from God, probably an angel. I don't think God the Father was talking to me. After all, even Mary was approached by an angel with a message from God. If the Father did not speak directly to Mary, I am confident He sent only a messenger to me. I don't know if who He sent was my guardian angel or some other angel.

The voice I heard during the miracles that happened when I was a lifeguard, a parent, and in the hospital was different from the voice from the vision in the red room. The former voice was caring and passionate, while the latter voice was indifferent; that is, until I was freed, and then I could sense relief in the voice.

God can ask regular people to carry messages as well. An example of an everyday messenger is the parishioner who told the priest in Pennsylvania that God told him to expect many visitors. Sometimes we are asked to say something to a friend, a family member, or maybe even a complete stranger. I believe that is the Holy Spirit's tapping us on the shoulder, nudging us to do our part.

As Christians, we shouldn't ignore those urgings. I've also learned to ask the Holy Spirit to help me whenever I give a talk or share my witness. The times I have forgotten to do so haven't gone nearly as well, but when I ask for help, the conversation flows more naturally, and I'm better able to focus my concentration.

As I reflected on my vision of Jesus on the cross, I began to understand how God exists outside of time as we experience it. The crucifixion and death of Jesus are seen by God simultaneously with each moment we sin. Jesus is not experiencing His Passion again—no, He did that once and for always. However, God views all of time at once. Jesus carries the pain of our sins (past, present, and future) from the garden of Gethsemane to the scourging and finally to the crucifixion because God is timeless. He has witnessed all of creation from its beginning to its end. He has seen every person from birth to death. Therefore, Jesus, being fully God and fully man, has seen the entirety of all creation, including our sins, and He carried them for us in His Passion.

We are transported to the Last Supper and to the crucifixion during the celebration of the Mass. We aren't only remembering and receiving His current body, blood, soul, and divinity, but we're traveling outside of time to celebrate the Last Supper, the death and resurrection of our Lord with all the saints on earth and in heaven. No clocks are hung in a Catholic Church because we are worshiping outside of time.

I used to wear a watch daily because I was a slave of time, in part due to the nature of my profession. Now time is less important to me, and my watch is only worn occasionally as jewelry—not as a master's chain. Much of my time before the wreck was spent on activities I now see were of little importance. I was building more treasures here and fewer treasures in the kingdom.

I now make a conscious effort to use my time to fulfill His will, but I know I can't do it on my own. I need Christ's guiding hand to be a constant help. In prayer, I ask that He help me to align my will with His, and I commit not to force my will upon the Lord. I'm confident that has never worked in all of history, so why keep trying? Following through with this plan is easier said than done though, and I find myself falling short regularly.

I've learned that the Lord often gives tasks that may be an interruption in my day, but doing God's work is far more important than mine and keeping on a tight schedule. I learned this truth from the actions of the compassionate nurse in the SDU, when he stopped his work and graciously said, "I have nothing else to do right now."

I've learned spending time reading Scripture and absorbing religious books and writings from saints is important. Every time I've had an aha moment or gained new understanding was because my memory was jogged by something I heard on a podcast or read in a book. For instance, St. Anne reminded me of my crucifixion dream. Some saints explain that when you are in prayer or reading and you experience a vision or deep inner thought, drop everything! Allow yourself to be immersed in that vision. Careful contemplation can help reveal an important truth or an answer to a prayer.

The visions of evil that I saw changed me. I am still very fearful when I recall the dark parts of that vision where I was trapped. I can't explain how or why I was terrified, but it made me aware of the effect of sin and evil. Sometimes I can sense evil in a person or a situation, or I may become aware of sin even in a person I don't know. Trust me, I'm not like Saint Padre Pio who could read souls; however, this experience of being close to the Holy Spirit seems to have made me more perceptive and aware of right and wrong, of truth and deceit, and of the lies of the Enemy. On the bright side, I always feel God's hand on my soul, which is immensely comforting. Sometimes I meditate only on feeling His touch.

Some close family members initially struggled with the dark parts of my story because of the misery it seemed to cause me. I thought perhaps I was being punished in the vision. Over time, I realized the vision of being trapped was intended to teach me to completely surrender myself to God because all the knowledge of the world wouldn't help me on my own. The important lesson is about His mercy—not about punishment. God is merciful, and God is love.

As I have already mentioned, I also understand now that the reason I could not pray in that place was because of God's absence. Our prayers spring forth from God, and without Him, we are unable to pray. I knew He was no longer with me, and I missed His touch. At the same time, I had no awareness that prayer existed or was an option. Nothing in this world can compare to the terror and pain of being separated from God.

Once when I was visiting Fr. Dale, I noticed a green binder covered with books and folders behind his desk to which I was strangely drawn. After leaving, my mind was still on its contents. The next time I met him, I told him I thought I was supposed to ask him if I could read it or have a copy. He was very kind to share. I could not believe that he had loaned me his notes on mysticism during his theological formation.

On the first page in the binder was a paragraph written by Fr. John Govan, S.J., who I'm told was a great educator of Christian spirituality on the subject of mystics. One page, which contained the explanation of the red room in my vision, was for me. In part, that paragraph read as follows:

Even though we grow up in the world and become adults, this is only the beginning. You have a shadow… Make friends with your shadow and become children of God once again. You need to start over and be in the process of being reborn by God. This second birth involves a process of purification and a new teaching by God. It begins in earnest when you experience an existential powerlessness that forces you to deal with your unconscious mind. As you are forced to look at unmoving obstacles, you are seeing your shadow truth and being asked by God, "Who do you say you are?" You are in the process of being transformed by God and being weaned of your attachments to have a more mature faith. You are being brought by God to realize and accept the fact of your humanity. You will admit that God is God, and you are not. The Law is being written on your heart, and God is moving into the center of your being.

Fr. Govan's writing seemed to be very relevant. I certainly had experienced existential powerlessness both in my vision and in my recovery. I had faced many unmoving obstacles and had my humanity staring at me in the face. I admitted that I was definitely not God and certainly not powerful without Him. Thankfully, He was moving to the center of my being. We must move through that lifelong process until we finally pass from this life to the next.

My understanding of the spiritual events in my life has evolved and may continue to evolve. This is true of our understanding of the faith. The faith, in and of itself does not change, but our understanding grows as we study throughout our lifetime, and as knowledge is passed down from one generation to another and through the Church as well.

When assembling a puzzle, we fit together a bunch of pieces and place them on the board where we think they belong. Once placed, it's sometimes obvious that the pieces didn't really belong in that spot. Those pieces were meant to be somewhere else. We have to keep on searching to find their perfect fit. Sure, we can leave them and try to force them into place, but the puzzle won't look as the artist intended.

Life is like a puzzle, and sometimes we try to "force issues" in the puzzle of our life. We put a few pieces together and place them where we think they should fit. We can even force them because we think they belong in that very spot. If we are aligning ourselves to God's will, we understand that we aren't assembling the puzzle; rather, God is! Therefore, we need to allow Him to complete the puzzle He's designing for us. I feel I only have the border and a couple of corners complete. God still has an abundance of work to do to help me fill in the rest!

"So, as you received Christ Jesus the Lord, walk in him, rooted in him and built upon him and established in the faith as you were taught, abounding in thanksgiving" (Colossians 2:6-7).

CHAPTER NINE

THE NEXT PIECE
OF THE PUZZLE

I RETURNED TO work at FedEx on April 6, 2020, nearly three years after my devastating car wreck. Because I was away for such a long time, I required a full-length training course to requalify as a pilot for the airline. I was very conflicted about returning to work. I felt that God had given me a great message that needed to be shared with everyone I could reach, and I wasn't sure that returning to work was what God wanted for me. I struggled with questions I needed answered:

- What were God's plans for my future?
- Could my body handle going back to flying?
- Did going back to my old job mean I was turning away from my new life perspective?
- Did God have a different plan for me?

I wrestled with these questions for months.

I felt I was given signs from the moment I arrived at the Indianapolis International Airport to catch my flight to Memphis for training—that I was being led to turn around and return home. Even though I was the only customer at the counter, checking my bag took 40 minutes. My connecting flight was canceled, and my luggage was lost. Once in my rental car, I was nearly broadsided on the highway by another driver the moment I entered the freeway. I saw the vehicle at the last second, and I missed being hit by inches. I was convinced God was giving me signs that I was on the wrong path.

After discussing all these "signs" with Amy, the next morning on my way to class, I told God I was going to speak to someone at FedEx about medically retiring. I arrived early to my first day of class and engaged in normal chitchat. Colleen, my instructor, who had been my training partner almost 15 years ago to the day when we were new hires, inquired about my accident, and as I explained what had happened, another presenter named Tom overheard us and told me of his own near-death experience. He started with the phrase, "There is no reason on earth why I should be here."

Tom shared how he had nearly been split in half in a boating accident almost 40 years earlier. When he arrived at the hospital, the doctors were amazed he was still alive. We shared our stories, and I was astonished by how many similarities we shared though our scenarios were entirely different.

More students filed in, and class finally started with a brief introduction given by the instructors and then by the students. One of the students named Grant mentioned that he had been out on medical leave for two years, and he ended his brief introduction with the statement: "God is very, very good!"

I immediately perked up at his exclamation involving God. I had been struggling for months as to what my next step should be. Medically, I knew I could have retired, and no one would have argued whether that was the right choice for me. At the same time, a big part of me wanted to try to come back to see how I would do with the long-term effects on my diminished body.

I had chosen to try to return to work but constantly prayed for my decision to be what God wanted of me—not what I wanted. When I arrived for training, I was positive I had chosen poorly. I hoped God would understand that I had simply made a mistake. I was sure I would find no sign of God at work, and that my path was meant to be outside of this career.

But on the very first morning of training, Grant mentioned praise for God, which is something I've never heard in the decades-worth of airline training I've completed. When my turn came, I gave a brief intro, including that I had been in a very bad head-on auto collision, and that I had taken three years to recover. I finished my summary with "God is great!" as I looked at Grant.

During our first break, I approached Grant and asked if he would share what the medical reason was for his long absence since he didn't mention it earlier. He proceeded to tell an impossible story of his unlikely survival, and his even less-likely return to work.

As Grant shared his story, he said, "There is no reason on earth why I should be here." There was that statement was again! I had already heard those very words once that morning from another pilot, who told of his miraculous survival. Within an hour, I had heard it twice. *Is this the sign I am looking for?* Grant hadn't yet arrived when Tom had told me his story that morning, so Grant was unaware that Tom had used the exact same phrase.

Grant then asked me why I was on medical leave. I told him of my collision, the resulting injuries and recovery, but I did not mention my spiritual experiences. When I finished, another student said, "Well, it sounds like you shouldn't be here either."

I replied, "There is no reason on Earth that I am here."

The class continued, and at one point, we took a personality test. I was surprised by my results, which stated that I was among less than one percent of the population who are categorized as an "Advocate," and then in parentheses appeared the word *Mystical.*

I had never been very comfortable with the title of this book, but now I thought, *Wow! Maybe my title did fit.* I simply stared at the results that described the form of evangelization I had been doing for the last 15 months or so. I was incredibly uncomfortable since the instructors published our results for the class to see. We discussed our listed traits as a group and how those traits would make us better leaders.

After listening to all the typical leadership descriptions of the other pilots who had the traits most people would associate with airline captains, my traits were then read last:

- "Able to know what others are thinking"
- "Discerning the underlying intentions of others"
- "Seeing the unseen"

Uncomfortable in the silence, I looked around the room. The

instructor typed my four-digit description code into the computer as he had done for the others so he could let us know what percentile of FedEx pilots I fell into. Then he said, "Huh? You're the first one of *those*."

Soon after when we took another break, Grant approached me in the hallway and said, "You weren't like that before the crash." I knew he was referring to the personality test results. He turned a little to look at the other people around us and waved his arm to encompass the room. "Ed, they don't know what is really important—that this isn't real."

At that point, I was sure of what I had felt earlier when I met Grant, so I said, "You had a spiritual experience, and I'd like to hear about it."

Grant immediately paused, and I knew that feeling. He was trying to talk but couldn't because he could feel God so strongly. Tears welled up in his eyes just as the Virgin Mary had told me they would flow for us when we are in the presence of our Lord.

He finally said, "I have never really told anyone about it, except once. I haven't even written it down." I told him I had written about my experience and that I happened to have a copy with me. I gave Grant an earlier edition of my book.

He read it that night. The following day at lunch, we sat in a corner as he quizzed me about various Bible verses. I knew he was testing me, perhaps to determine if I might be a person with whom he might share his experience. After school that day, I returned to my rental car with a newfound excitement.

At the end of that first day, I sat in my car, prayed, and

thanked God for leading me there. I thanked Him for showing me what this new path looked like. I thanked Him for giving me a priest who understood the mystical side of our faith and who encouraged and helped me to understand what I had seen. I thought about the odds of having three near-death experiences sitting in the same room in the FedEx Training Center. I laughed to myself thinking of the people, even my fellow students, who call God's guiding hand a coincidence. I thanked Him for guiding Grant to say those surprising words during his introduction.

Grant and I shared lunch again a few weeks later, and he shared his amazing story with me. We were moving on to a phase of training that would have us going our own ways.

As I left our lunch, I let Grant know what part he had played in my decision to stay at FedEx and complete my retraining. I told him that his simple testimony, "God is very, very good" was exactly what I needed to hear at that moment. I explained that when he had said those words, I felt that nudge from the Holy Spirit, Who told me I was listening to a soul who had experienced God's personal touch. "Grant, after that first day of training, I sat in my car and gave a prayer of thanksgiving. I realized that I was not being led by God to turn away and go back home. I was being led away from where God wanted me to go, and I was being shown fear and doubt by a spirit of the enemy."

My understanding that spirits are working against us was a great lesson for me to grasp. Unlike our guardian angels, these fallen angels desire for us to move against God's will. The Holy Spirit nudges us all the time to say or do a small insignificant act, but how often do we listen? Who are we to determine if our words are insignificant?

When I was first cleared to go back to work, I waited over a month for a training slot. As friends discovered I was back and waiting, they would ask, "Are you excited?" During my wait, I had to go into FedEx a couple of times for administration items, and I met folks there as well asking the same question. I met other pilots at the hotel the night before training started, also with the same question, and in my mind, the answer was no, I wasn't excited. I felt that I was not doing God's will and was on a dead-end path for spreading God's Word.

Thank God, Grant listened to that urge to say five simple words that would change the course of my life and keep me on God's chosen path. I pray we all say the words God asks us to speak.

On May 31, 2020, three years and one day after my near-death accident, I completed my training and passed my required test called a "check ride" to return as a captain to FedEx. Yes, God is very, very good!

God wants us to share our stories about Him with one another. Mystical stories or faith experiences shouldn't be taboo any longer. We are all mystics, and we can all be in touch with God. Your story may not be as dramatic as mine. Perhaps a new believer or unbeliever may have an easier time relating to a less dramatic story, a small sign, or a "God wink" as a friend likes to call them. Don't be afraid to tell your friends or even a stranger about how God has blessed or helped you.

———

Who is God? Many people think of God as a Spirit somewhere "out there" in the heavens. I want to share my experience to show that God is physically real; that after He saved my life, He touched me with His Spirit; and He holds my soul in His hand. God is a real, tangible, touchable, caring Being. I physically experienced joy and bliss from God which is so much more powerful than anything on earth. The more I surrender to God's will in my life, the more joy I feel in doing so. God isn't, "out there" somewhere; rather, He dwells within us in our soul.

Since God is real and touches us, miracles are also real and happen every day. Saints have been talking about miracles for ages, but many of us pretend miracles are not a part of our world or in our time. My life has been full of miracles. Opening our eyes to God and His voice will open us up to more miracles that occur around us.

I tell this story so that you who read it can understand that God speaks to us and works through us every day. I want you to reflect on your own life and remember those times when our Lord has spoken to you or guided you. I pray that you may awaken to the Lord's will and share your stories with others so that we may all work to seek out and lead lost souls to Christ's salvation.

Unfortunately, after 22 months back flying, I was forced once again to hang up my wings, but this time it was for good. The remaining damage and physical stress of the job took too much of a toll on my diminished body. Despite everything I have been through, I know I am truly blessed and truly loved.

———

I know I am never alone. I know He has a plan for me, as He does for you. I know God will lead me where I need to be, and I am truly thankful for the opportunities He provides.

As often as you can, share your own story of God with others and spread the good news of our risen Lord!

I began this story as a man who thought he was on his way to heaven because my paltry efforts were enough to enter His kingdom of heaven. I end it knowing that, as a child of God, I am called to love the Lord with all my heart and soul and to love my neighbor as myself. And now I know that even if I do my best to obey those commandments, it is only through the mercy of Jesus Who said, *"I am the way and the truth and the life. No one comes to the Father except through me"* (John 14:6), that I will come to enter the kingdom.

Wishing you blessings, calm winds, and blue skies.

Then I heard the voice of the LORD saying, "Whom shall I send? Who will go for us?" "Here I am," I said; "send me!" (Isaiah 6:8).

GLOSSARY OF TERMS

Anointing of the Sick

A sacrament administered in times of sickness or near death, to bring spiritual and physical strength. Instituted by Jesus during His earthly ministry (cf. Mark 6:13, James 5:14-15).

Blessed Sacrament

The Blessed Sacrament is the Body, Blood, Soul, and Divinity of Christ which becomes present when the priest prays the prayers of consecration at Mass.

Catechism

The Catechism summarizes 2,000 years of the Catholic Christian faith. It contains the Catholic doctrine of morals, faith, and the whole of the Church's tradition. The primary sources are the Sacred Scriptures, the Church Fathers, the Liturgy, and the Church's Magisterium. To be catechized is to know and understand the content of the Catechism (abbreviated as CCC).

Catechized

From the root word *catechesis*. Another word for teaching.

Father

Title of ordained Catholic priests to indicate they are a spiritual father (1 Corinthians 4:15).

Mass

"At the Last Supper, on the night he was betrayed, our Savior instituted the Eucharistic Sacrifice of his Body and Blood. He did this in order to perpetuate the sacrifice of the cross throughout the centuries until He should come again, and so to entrust to His beloved spouse, the Church, a memorial of His death and resurrection: a sacrament of love, a sign of unity, a bond of charity, a paschal banquet in which Christ is consumed, the mind is filled with grace, and a pledge of future glory is given to us" (Sacrosanctum Concilium 47).

Monstrance

An ornate vessel *(pictured right)* used to display the Blessed Sacrament, (Jesus' Eucharistic presence in the Host), for prayer and adoration.

Purgatory

"All who die in God's grace and friendship, but still imperfectly purified, are indeed assured of their eternal salvation; but after death they undergo purification, so as to achieve the holiness necessary to enter the joy of heaven." (CCC1030)

"The Church gives the name Purgatory to this final purification of the elect, which is entirely different from the punishment of the damned." (CCC1032 [Ref: 1 Peter 3:19, 1 Corinthians 3:15, 2 Maccabees 12:43–45]).

Rosary

A collection of prayers said repetitiously while simultaneously meditating on the mysteries of Jesus' birth, life, death, and Resurrection. The use of rosary beads helps to keep track of the order of prayers, thus allowing the mind and body to perform the prayer together. It is a devotion that asks the Holy Mother Mary to intercede for with her Son, for the intentions of our prayers, as she did for the bride and groom at the Wedding at Cana (John 2:1-12). While the prayer is called the Rosary, Catholics often call the beads the Rosary as well, but the correct name is rosary beads.

ACKNOWLEDGMENTS

I MUST FIRST thank God for the untold miracles He lavished and continues to lavish upon me.

Thanks to…

- My family and friends who have cared for me and spent so much of their time with me.

- The church groups, friends, and neighbors who fed my family when I couldn't.

- The medical personnel, who through God's grace, saved what was impossible to save.

- All the faithful around the country who prayed for me all the days of my recovery.

A special thanks to my friend and priest, Father Dale Ehrman, for walking with me on this journey and for his guidance in helping me to understand the messages God has given to me.

To Lori Lowe, for her writing assistance in helping me tell this story, for asking me the tough questions that made me dig deeper, and for allowing the Holy Spirit to work through us.

My deep appreciation also goes to Sharron Wright for her graphic design expertise in creating the original printed book, enabling my story to reach so many.

Printed in the USA
CPSIA information can be obtained
at www.ICGtesting.com
LVHW021307240324
775372LV00003B/300